T0156798

Class of TWO THOUSAND SOMETHING

From A Freshmen To A Graduating Senior While Surviving the Process as Painlessly as Possible.

Dechele Byrd

iUniverse, Inc.

New York   Bloomington

iUniverse books may be ordered through booksellers or by contacting:

iUniverse
1663 Liberty Drive
Bloomington, IN 47403
www.iuniverse.com
1-800-Authors (1-800-288-4677)

ISBN: 978-1-4401-2869-1 (sc)
ISBN: 978-1-4401-2868-4 (ebook)

Printed in the United States of America

iUniverse rev. date: 04/01/2009

Table of Contents

Acknowledgements

This book was generated through a lot of thoughts from people in my life over the years. I would first like to thank the most high GOD. As I continue to discover the source and the meaning of my life I have truly manifested into a fantastic being that loves to find new ways to give. Thank you for continuing to answer the questions I have about becoming a better person in life.

I must continue to find many ways of giving thanks for my parents: Zelda, Eddie, and Danny. Each of you have given me something that I value each day. It takes two to create life. It takes just one to shape a life. Remember the value that you give to others even in the smallest of ways.

To my siblings who I love so dearly because you all have been a part of me and have given me mental exams of what it takes to succeed. You are forever my loves.

To my editors for all the work you put into making sure that my work was clearly stated and understood. I have to say a very special thanks to David. The breakfast meetings were the best! We must do it again sometime soon.

To my publishing company I express deep gratitude for getting this project completed and distributed by my target goal. I send many thanks to you and your prosperity.

My cousin Mona, I want to thank you for great inspiration and being the messenger to remind me that I have something to write about and share to the world. The dreams are endless for all who wish to challenge themselves to be the best. Thanks for being an example of greatness.

To any and everyone that has contributed in some form or way to my life whether it be a great or greater contribution. I am learning the lessons of life everyday, and it wouldn't have been this fun so far if it weren't for your contribution to my life.

To the alumni, students and staff of Westchester High School and especially the real "W" WASHINGTON PREPARATORY HIGH SCHOOL. I learned so much about high school both as a student and as an administrator. The experiences are invaluable to me. I hope that I was able to capture how to receive all the wonderful moments that I was given during my time at both schools. Especially receive the ones that cause you to grow into being the very best you can be in life. Prep N' Generals is an example of greatness giving back to the source. This book is yet another!

I want to thank the total inspiration of my life, my beautiful daughter Yanai. You are the reason your mother is reminded to work to make herself better in every way. This book shows you that anything you desire to do in life can be done. Always accept the very best because you are my Pretty Princess and because you have gifts that must be used to share with the world. I LOVE YOU my Pretty Pooh!

Introduction

Being an educator has afforded me with many opportunities to see the possibilities of what students can become. I am a living example of successfully navigating through the process called high school. However, the most important thing is that I have learned how to travel through the fanatical system of public and private education sectors through the post secondary graduate school level.

My experience with this process called High School was both rewarding and enlightening. Now I watch the average youth feverishly attempt to master being a student in a school system that is built upon values and resources that are Jurassic in comparison to the students of today's available technology resources. In addition, the portrayal of students of today is grossly inaccurate, and better yet, students are truly misunderstood. I often hear teachers say, "Students of today don't care about school," or "Students are different from when I was in school," yet they neglect to remember the times when they were once thought of as careless rebels because of the new available things in their lives.

As a student in high school I had the time of my life enjoying friends, preparing for college, and creating life-long relationships that are still thriving today because of the Internet. High school was an experience where I was able to take pride in my work and deliver my best performance knowing that I would be celebrated by my inner feelings and other's recognition.

As an administrator in an urban high school similar to the school I attended, I witnessed the same levels of drive from students who had pride in their work and enjoyed the presence of other students, faculty, and staff. The changes that I see are very minimal in that all students want is someone who cares about their lives and the direction it takes.

In conversations I often ponder the thought of why my experience in high school was so positive, and one common thread that exists is that someone assisted me when I needed to believe in myself. Collectively we cared about being the best, so nothing else mattered.

The reality for today's student is an educational system that operates like a nervous system trying to fight a disease: the students are like the white blood cells that are fighting of the toxins that are given by the red blood cells before they are deposited to the brain. The toxins are outside influences of the media, lack of consistent parenting, and the ills of the world causing the white cells to slowly die off and no longer be able to fight the disease.

Being a high school student is not so difficult once you have the right idea in mind. And being a parent or guardian of a student in high school can be even more rewarding as you become a better advocate for your child. We all learn something new every day, which makes us all life-long learners or better know as lifetime students. What lessons are we learning that will create a better life for all? Many lessons that are being taught focus so much on the negative aspects of life. We are bombarded with the drop-out rates and failing rates of our students. Through this book my goal is to clear the road so that everyone can access a clear path to learn and to learn the right lessons to earn a diploma at a high school graduation and eventually earn a degree, certificate or credentials desired to live out their life dreams.

I have been asked many questions over the years from students, family and friends about how to graduate from high school; what classes to take; how to find out more about college; how and when to register for the SAT; the advantages of taking an advanced placement course; why are these classes required – just to name a few. These questions are answered throughout this book as I explain how I survived high school and you can too!

The ultimate goal with the completion of high school is to provide society with the greatest possible contribution from you through your career choices. In the United States you are provided with free education from kindergarten through the twelfth grade. Take advantage of receiving this gift by engulfing yourself with the many opportunities to learn and grow.

My goal for this book is to provide students with some basic steps to doing their very best in high school; to provide students with ways to develop and excel or to catch themselves when they fail; to provide parents with some tools that will help them to understand school as a parent not as a student going through the system from the past; and finally to build a league of students who are demonstrating the attributes of greatness.

Let's begin the journey... CLASS OF TWO THOUSAND SOMETHING: From A Freshmen To A Graduating Senior While Surviving the Process as Painlessly as Possible.

9th Grade Year!

The ninth grade year is the most critical year in high school because this year is a time when you must tackle the basics of your academic classes, establish a strong foundation and plan to complete your work, and find your way around the campus. It is also a time when you discover exactly what you are truly interested in doing for potential careers. The ninth grade year, also called the freshmen year, is a serious year because you want to make your high school career the most successful one possible.

As you start the ninth grade year, you should know the expectations to receive a high school diploma. When you know the criteria in the beginning, it helps to you to create a plan of action. In public high schools around the nation there are minimum requirements to earn a high school diploma.

In most states you must take the following courses: four years of English; two or three years of mathematics with Algebra and Geometry being required; two or three years of social science; two or three years of science including physical and biological science; one or more years of physical education; one or more years of a technical elective course, one or more years of visual or performing art elective. Some states also require students to complete a course related to health and personal development skills.

The basics of school is simple, every student starts the first day of school with an "A." The key is to maintain that "A" for the rest of the year. A majority of students don't seem to know exactly what to do to keep the top grade, however, when you follow the steps outlined in this book, it becomes simple to do. There are just a few steps that are necessary in order to maintain a 4.0 GPA.

In your freshman year, you will take 1 year of English, 1 year of Algebra I or a higher level of math, 1 year of introductory Physical Science, 1 year of an elective, 1 year of physical education, a semester of health education and a semester of life skills or another personal development type elective course. Completion of each course will give you enough credits to move forward to the next grade level.

There are certain rules a freshman must follow to be successful in high school: be in class on time, do your work in class, complete homework, study for tests and exams, and get involved in activities to make your high school career the best possible experience. In this year you are introduced to lunch time dances, pep rallies, spirit week activities, homecoming celebrations, and many exciting events that happen at high school. With all of these fun activities it is important to have a good balance between socialization and academics.

Part of enjoying your high school experience requires you to be a proactive student. A proactive student takes being in class seriously by knowing the difference between participating in class and just going to class. Participating requires you to ask questions when you don't understand, restate what is said to clarify what you understand, describe what you understand to the best of your ability, and share the results with the right people at the right time.

Get to know your administrators in a positive way. Administrators include the Principal, Assistant Principals, and Dean. They are very approachable and love to make a connection with students in a good way. Take a moment in the first week to know who is in charge of everything you will need to maximize your learning. Formally introduce yourself to your teachers at the end of each class period. Let them know something about you in order to establish a connection with them. The more the teacher can personalize something with you the more easily you will relate to them and their instruction. Perhaps writing a letter to each of your teachers would be a good strategy to achieve this goal.

In 9th grade English and Math are the only two academic classes that count toward your college transcript, but don't let that confuse you into thinking that the rest of your classes are meaningless. The other classes are preparation for academic requirements that will help you to pass the state required exit exam or competency test, and to receive competitive scores on the **Preliminary Scholastic Aptitude Test (PSAT), Explore, Scholastic Aptitude Test (SAT) I (Reasoning) and SAT II (Subject Test), and/or the American College Test (ACT).**

You may have heard about or even taken the PSAT in 8th grade. This test is given annually on one Wednesday and Saturday in October. I encourage you to take it every year so that you are well prepared by your senior year to take the SAT. This test measures your ability to score well on the SAT. There is another test preparation by the ACT called Explore that is now being offered to students in the 8th and 9th grades. There is a nominal fee to take each test. I strongly suggest you take the preparation test every time it is offered so that you become familiar with taking tests on a regular basis. This will prevent you from the anxiety that comes along with taking tests. For more information about the ACT or Explore visit www.act.org, and for more information about the PSAT or the SAT I and II visit www.collegeboard.com.

In the spring semester of your 9th grade year you must prepare to get involved in some type of activity. Many opportunities are available to all students in athletics, clubs, organizations, or volunteer class projects. Join student council or leadership; try out for an athletic team like volleyball, soccer, tennis, basketball, or golf. This is the best time to learn a new activity for free. You may even be competitive enough to earn team awards and athletic divisional recognition. Consider trying out for cheerleading, drill team, or a spirit squad. If you play an instrument or are interested in music, there is always choir and band. If you are an actress or actor, then drama club and class is the way to enhance your skills. There are many chances for you to show your talents and develop new ones. Take a risk to show how great you are by truly getting involved.

Getting involved helps you become a more well-rounded student and it surrounds you with goal-oriented people. These activities will also require you to maintain a required G.P.A. as you are on your road to greatness.

Ways to Excel:

Near the end of your successful 9th grade year you must begin to challenge yourself to do more for your education to reach your goals. Schedule a meeting with your counselor to take honors level courses. These courses are more rigorous classes with an increased amount of expectation. You may also receive additional points on your weighted average for determining your overall GPA. This challenges and prepares you to take advanced placement courses and college level courses.

In the 9th grade you take an elective class. Make it a foreign language course so that you have the opportunity to take three or more levels during high school. This is a great way for colleges to see that you are a serious student, and it gives you the communication skills to speak with others from another country whose language is different from English.

Because you have followed the suggestions in this book, summer school is not required. Instead enroll in a summer institute through a local college or university. These programs count as outside activities for your college application requirements or college unit credit.

Troubleshooting:

What do you do if you didn't pass all of your classes?

I am concerned that you may not have followed my advice about getting to know your teachers and completing all of your work. Be sure you understand what you are learning and remember to always ask for help from anyone that is willing to help you I would suggest you begin by speaking with your counselor immediately. Make an appointment as quickly as you can to discuss ways to progress to the next grade. Also, ask about the various tutoring options available to you.

I earned a "D" in my English (or Algebra) class, what should I do?

Earning a "D" is totally unsatisfactory and will not count towards your college entrance credits. Before you finish the eleventh grade you must re-take any "D" earned on your final semester grades. You can re-take a course during summer school, but space may be limited. It would be easier to complete the class when it is currently assigned, instead of having to take it during summer school.

I tried out for a team or a spirit squad and I didn't make it. What should I do now?

First, remember it is not the end of the world - although it may feel that way initially. I suggest finding something else you are interested in and go after that activity. Doing this will keep you busy with determination and occupy your time with the right kind of activities.

10th Grade Year!

In the tenth grade you are able to spread your wings because you are no longer the new student on campus. You have successfully completed all of your courses from the ninth grade while you continue to work toward your college entrance requirements. Of all the years in high school, this year may be the most challenging for several reasons. You will take the most academic courses (5) in a school year, you will take the PSAT, you will take and pass the High School Exit Exam, (if applicable in your state), you are now more involved in activities at your school, and you have more responsibilities.

First and foremost, you will take the most academic courses at one time during the 10th grade year. Five of the six classes you will have count towards the college entrance requirements. The academic courses you should be taking are: English, Geometry or another higher level mathematics, World History, Biology, an elective (visual and performing arts, technical art, or foreign language), and physical education. That means during this year your grade point average (GPA) will include the calculations from the grades you receive from five of the courses to determine your eligibility for acceptance to a university or college. Physical education is not calculated into your GPA for colleges; however, it is calculated as a graduation requirement and must be passed in order to receive your diploma. This is why you must really do your very best in all subjects to increase your GPA and marketability as an incoming college freshman.

In October of your 10th grade year, you will have an opportunity to take the PSAT, which prepares you for the SAT I. This test gives a strong indication on how well you will do when you take the SAT, which you will take by the first semester of your senior year. The PSAT has My College QuickStart™ that can be accessed from the College Board website at www.collegeboard. com to help you plan your career and determine your interests based upon the questions that you answer correctly. You will get a score report by the spring following the test that reviews each test question you answered correctly and incorrectly with an explanation. For more information about the PSAT or SAT you can visit www.collegeboard. com and for the ACT visit www.act.org.

In most states you are able to take the high school exit exam for the first time in your sophomore year. This is the exam that will determine if you are qualified to receive a high school diploma the state in which you live. It tests you on skills you have acquired from first grade through the 8th grade making your time in elementary and middle school count for something more than just the certificates. The exit exam is given at various times in the year.

In the State of California, it is given in March of your 10th grade year and tests you in English/Language Arts and Mathematics. There is a writing portion on the exam as well. Your goal is to score 350 or above in both categories of the exam. However, in order to receive a proficient score, you must score at 380 or above.

Throughout your sophomore year there are many times to enjoy various events and activities. In the fall there is the homecoming dance or perhaps you are playing girl's soccer, running cross country, or playing an instrument in the band. The weeks leading to the homecoming game are usually filled with fun events to celebrate being a student. Maybe you are in leadership and helped to plan these great events. What activities are you participating in that will make you a very strong candidate for the college of your choice or prepare you for a great career doing something you love to do every day? If you haven't already made the decision to become more involved in activities at school, I encourage you to do so now! The other alternative to get involved is to join activities in your community through church or civic organization. Become a Girl or Boy scout, volunteer at a hospital, work at a local precinct during the elections, or sing in a choir to name just a few.

Ways to Excel:

Visit www.collegeboard.com on a regular basis to review your progress throughout high school based upon your scores on the PSAT. This tool can assist with determining areas of need that you may focus on to improve your scores on the SAT I.

When planning your class schedule for the eleventh grade, you should consider taking advanced placement courses in English, History and/or Science. The grades in these courses are calculated on a weighted average and receive 1.0 additional credit for a grade of "C" or higher. This could boost your grade point average to above a 4.0 GPA.

Also take an advanced math course like Algebra II, Trigonometry/Math Analysis, Calculus and/or Statistics. The more prepared you are by taking high level courses the more you are able to market yourself to colleges, universities and career programs.

Continue with the foreign language course that was suggested before. This will give you the second level of the language and reinforce what you have already learned.

Many local colleges have summer institutes or summer school courses available to high school students. Enroll in these courses to earn extra credits and/or college units toward your college degree.

Troubleshooting:

I didn't earn all my credits for the past two years. What do I do now?

This is a difficult time for you to face because you now have a decision to make. First you need to determine what is preventing you from passing all of your classes. If it is determined that the cause is related to motivation, then I would suggest you consider an alternative school setting that meets your needs more efficiently. Some students elect to attend a continuation school, a home studies program, or the Alternative Education Work and Career Centers. These options all work towards earning a high school diploma, require the passage of the high school exit exam, provide ways for students to complete their courses in a shorter period of time, and have a large graduation to celebrate the accomplishment of earning a diploma.

I don't want to leave my friends behind what should I do?

Let us be honest you have demonstrated you are not capable of doing your very best with the distraction of your friendships around campus. A change in school settings could be just what you need in order to start fresh. A new start always makes your perspective on life much better, so embrace the need for change as a consequence for your choices.

11th Grade Year!

Eleventh grade was the most fun of all the years in high school to me because I had a lot of great experiences as a student in the classroom, and there were a lot of events that brought me closer to my classmates.

During the 11th grade year you will take courses that are more advanced and more interesting. This is a time in your life when you should be thinking about how to finance your senior year, prepare for the SAT or ACT, and make some specific choices about colleges or career preparation. You will start to feel more mature and comfortable as a student making decisions that are more relevant to your future plans.

This year is still very critical and the majority of the courses you will take are calculated into your GPA. Because you have learned the techniques to balance studying and socializing, your year should be great. In the eleventh grade you will take American Literature and Contemporary Composition as English courses. You are encouraged to take advanced mathematics even though high schools require only two years of mathematics to receive a diploma. This is the year you will continue to learn in more detail about the United States of America as you build on what you learned in grades five and eighth. Chemistry is the science that is required and should be taken in connection with Algebra II. Many of the concepts you will learn are tied together to make critical points and conclusions. Physical education is no longer required; however, if you followed good advice and joined a team sport, you will continue on with practice and league competition as a class during one of the semesters. You also have another elective course similar to your choices in the 9th and 10th grades. This is a great time to take a language course or some type of specialty course offered at your school.

In the eleventh grade you are typically 16 years old, which makes you eligible to hold a work permit and work up to 20 hours per week. With your senior year approaching, many costs are associated with the fun and excitement of school. It would be great for you to work to contribute to paying for some of these activities. Take time during your eleventh grade year to identify the costs of things you would like to participate in during your final year of school. There are special things that will make your senior year memorable like: homecoming, prom, senior portraits, graduation announcements, the senior picnic, the senior breakfast, just to name a few. These events are fun yet can become very costly. Having a job to create a savings will make this fun and reduce the strain it may have on your family. You must only consider having a job if you have maintained good grades. In order to receive a work permit you have to maintain a 2.0 grade point average and have satisfactory attendance in school. Many schools will allow you to receive high school credits for students who are employed. Speak with your counselor for more information.

You will have another opportunity to pay for the PSAT in preparation of the SAT. At the conclusion of your eleventh grade year I suggest you take the SAT during the June administration to gauge your test results. These scores may be sufficient for you to enter college or you may want to study more to increase your score. On the College Board website at www.collegeboard.com or the ACT website at www.act.org, you can review specifics about your college goals. If you are planning to attend a State University it would benefit you to also take the Early Assessment Program (EAP) exam to determine if you are ready for college level mathematics and English/language arts.

Narrow your choices for the colleges, universities, or careers you are considering for post-secondary options. Schedule tours by signing up in your college/counseling office or through the outreach program advisors at the colleges. There are several tour companies that will provide you with visitations to various campuses across the country. These are paid tours that include travel and accommodations.

Consider what you love to do the most and develop a career from that choice. This will guarantee you will have a love for working each day while taking care of your responsibilities in life. Sign up to listen to speakers from various colleges. Attend workshops and college recruitment events. When selecting a college, know the specific requirements for earning a degree.

If college is not in your plans, there are many career options available to you. There are various training programs that can prepare you for a successful career, but most involve some type of post-secondary schooling.

For instance, if you want to work in the health care profession you must take courses that will prepare you to work with patients.

It is possible to have a successful and lucrative career without a college degree; however, it is necessary to have some formal training that will allow you to become certified in your field of expertise. Find a person in your future profession to shadow during their working hours so that you are clear on the responsibilities for completing the job. A person in the field is able to tell you specifically what you need to do to make this your career.

As a high school student, you may have the opportunity to do an internship or take classes toward college units or certifications through adult education programs. Remember you have an academic counselor and be sure to communicate your desires with them so they may guide you in the right direction.

Way to Excel:

If you haven't already scheduled to take an advanced placement course, do so now! Your senior schedule is not as demanding because you only have two courses required to receive your diploma. Take advantage of this light schedule by taking an advanced placement course in English, Government, Economics, Science or Math. Take the exams for each advanced placement course you complete. When you pass with a score of 3 or higher, the course counts towards a college requirement. Check with the college about graduation unit requirements in college to earn a degree. This will allow you to take more elective courses in college giving you more opportunities to explore many career options.

Join your school's Senior Steering Committee so that you are a part of shaping your graduation and senior events. Your opinion counts so make your voice heard by attending meetings and voting to make the important decisions.

Again, the summer institutes are available along with classes in the local community colleges that will give you an advantage over other candidates for colleges and careers. If you have taken the advice and enrolled in the summer institutes or courses at the college for the past three years, you could have up to 18 units (the equivalent of 1 full semester of college) that could be applied towards your college degree or certificate program moving you closer to the career of your dreams.

Establish a relationship with the admission director or faculty members at the college or university of your choice. This is a great way to let the faculty get to know more about you. Attend tours and presentations offered throughout the end of your junior year and the beginning of your senior year.

Troubleshooting:

I haven't joined any clubs or organizations will I still get into college?

Being involved in activities are necessary for entrance into most colleges or universities. Recruiters are looking for well-rounded students who have a lot of experience working with others. These activities will demonstrate that you are able to apply both academic and social skills successfully.

Begin by taking an inventory of the things you like to do. Take that list and find activities that are in alignment. For example: if you enjoy singing join the choir or participate in "caroling" during the holidays; if you like shopping volunteer to be a personal shopper for an elderly person or a disabled family; or if you like to hangout with friends why not volunteer to be a poll worker during an election or assist with evening events at your school?

I don't have much money to spare on taking things like the PSAT, getting a tutor, or college applications, what should I do?

In the 9th grade I told you how important it is to get to know the adults on your campus. This is a time when you can put those relationships to work. Begin with your counselor who is capable of directing you to all types of resources and fee waivers for various tests if you qualify for the National School Lunch Porgram. For more information about this free or reduce meal program visit www.fns.usda.gov/cnd/lunch/.

If you are not qualified under the federal meal plan criteria and you are still unable to afford the fees, speak with your administrators. Often there are special funds available for students who have hardship circumstances. Many are considered on a case-by-case basis. Always be proactive in using the resources you have available to you. A financial hardship also includes funding for extracurricular activities like dances and social events for students who maintain a certain grade point average.

12th Grade Year!

Senior year has finally arrived! You should be extremely proud that you have made it this far by completing twelve or more years of school. CONGRATULATIONS on completing all your course work through this point! Although your course load is a lot lighter during your senior year, the subjects you take are relevant and very important.

In the 9th grade you were introduced to more responsibilities and more social opportunities at high school that were extremely fun and exciting. As a sophomore you demonstrated that you have what it takes to master and build your grade point average to be a competitive and well-rounded student. Your junior year was filled with fun activities and more interesting academic courses that help to shape your choices for college and careers. Now you are a masterful SENIOR who is prepared to apply for college and financial aid, take placement exams, and enjoy all types of senior activities.

Your senior year comes with a reduction of academic responsibilities, which causes a lack in motivation as the spring semester approaches. Students are required to complete 6 classes including Expository Composition and an English elective like World Literature, English Literature, or Myths and Legends. You should take another level of math although you may choose another elective. You must complete Government and Economics as high school graduation requirements. The remaining three courses can be split between various options: college level courses (off site and on site if available), advanced academic elective courses (Physics,

Trigonometry, or Speech), Regional Occupation Program (ROP) courses, or athletic teams.

By October you should be prepared to take the SAT and/or the ACT exams for entrance into college. If you are planning to attend a junior college these exams are not required, but are highly suggested as you may decide to transfer to a university as a sophomore student.

Junior colleges are a great way for students to begin their post secondary education. Classes at a junior college are rigorous and exciting, yet they are very inexpensive in comparison to a state college, state university, or private college. The fees for classes in the state of California are $20 per unit for in-state residents and $173 per unit for out-of-state residents. Seniors in high school may choose to attend a junior college to better prepare themselves for a university or to save on expenses.

The choice to attend a college or university is one that takes serious consideration if you followed the tips in this book, you are prepared.

Post-secondary education is an investment in your future. I encourage you to make choices that are carefully planned and will fit your needs for many years to come.

How are you going to pay for college or career preparation? You must complete the Free Application for Federal Student Aid, also known as the FAFSA by March 2. Complete the forms beginning in January to apply for scholarship, grants, and student loans for both two year and four year colleges and universities. You can find out more information by visiting www.fafsa.ed.gov on how to apply for financial aid. There is a lot of free money available to you so also visit websites like www.fastweb.com or www.schoolsoup.com to match your interests with scholarship and grant money opportunities.

While looking at funding for college and career programs you also must consider funding senior activities. Your senior portraits are an expensive treat that captures your happiness and smile in a cap and gown. You can share these pictures with people who are important in your life.

Most schools have a senior package that typically includes admission to most of the senior events and graduation materials (i.e. announcements, cap and gown, diploma covers, class rings, and the senior book.) The packages are designed to fit any budget, though they still can be very costly. The biggest event during your senior year outside of graduation is the Senior Prom. This event is an elegant night culminating four years of fun and exciting things both personally and academically. Tickets for the prom typically range from $60-120 per ticket. Outfit, transportation, and pre-prom parties are often expensive; however, with good planning and advanced preparation you can cut expenses down significantly.

All that is left during your senior year is to receive your college acceptance letters or job offers, your financial aid award letters, and complete your classes with exceptional grades for the remaining few months of school. Be sure to mail your graduation announcements to the people you love by the end of April. Seating is very limited at most graduation ceremonies so you need to make a decision on who will attend. Enjoy each and every moment of this time because the end of high school marks a new beginning in life. No longer will you, the student, be required by others to do things in school. Post-secondary activities become something you have to have the motivation to complete. The final thing you need to do during your senior year is to shake the hand of the principal and turn your tassel to the side. Congratulations!

Things You Should Know!

The basics of school are very simple if you follow my plan:

Every student starts the first day of school with an "A" in each class. A majority of students don't seem to know exactly what to do to keep the "A," but it is an easy task. In order to maintain a 4.0 GPA or above make an effort to arrive to all of your classes on time. Being punctual leaves the impression that you are committed to your education.

The best kept secret on a high school campus is the counselor. There are some key things that must happen for all students in high school to ensure that the transition from middle school is very smooth. The main person to connect with is your counselor. Each student is assigned a counselor during high school that typically will continue with you throughout the entire four years. Be sure to let your counselor know the things that interest you so that he or she may get a better idea of how to guide you to succeed.

If you are having problems in any area (academically or socially), your counselor can be your first defense. Counselors are able to handle all types of problems that you may not be comfortable talking about with your family or friends. They are able to connect you with many resources that can be of benefit in your life. So remember to meet with your counselor at least twice per year.

Each year beginning in the 2nd grade, students across the country take state mandated tests. These tests are used in a variety of ways and are representative of the instruction that is taking place in the classroom. The eleventh grade is the final grade tested in these state mandated tests.

In most states, the Standards Test covers the subjects of English/language arts, mathematics, social science, and science. There is a writing component in various grades including the 7th grade. Typically the test is measured by proficiency levels with "Advanced" being the highest and Far Below Basic being the lowest level. The scores measure the Annual Yearly Performance of school and are used to determine national rankings of similar schools.

When the test is offered you should find ways to take some additional preparation courses to improve your test taking skills. You will continue to be tested in every aspect of your life so it is best to become comfortable with this fact in order to do your very best.

There are test taking tips that can be used for any exam or standardized test. Here are a few examples:

- Get plenty of rest the

night before the test.

- Provide your body with energy by eating a healthy meal before the test.

- Be sure you understand the directions.

- Relax and take one question at a time.

- If you come to a question you don't know mark it and then move on to the next question.

- Read the entire question before you select an answer.

- Use the elimination process to select the best answer when you need to guess.

- Have confidence in yourself by repeating a positive affirmation.

- Follow your instincts when answering a question you will usually be right.

- Pay close attention to the

wording of the questions.

Your next ally for being the best student possible is your teachers. It is important to make a mental note about your teachers' personalities. Just like each of your friends has a distinct personality so does each of your teachers. Once you understand your teachers' personalities you can decide which approach is the best way to communicate. If your teacher likes to have things quiet, then follow that direction. When you have a question always write it down so that you have it as a point of reference. Don't take up too much time trying to be seen by continuing to raise your hand and getting upset when the teacher doesn't answer your questions right away. Write your question down and be prepared to ask someone who can answer the question in the best way you will learn.

What are your options if you need extra help? Some students have special designations that identify them with special needs to succeed in the classroom. Primarily, differentiated instruction is necessary for this type of person. A student could be classified as gifted or high achieving in one or more academic areas; support services are necessary in order to maximize learning opportunities; special classes and teachers are assigned so that students can receive more direct instruction with the help of an assistant. All these classifications allow students to take advantage of the additional resources that are available to do your very best. If you have a special designation, this section is just for you.

It is important for you to maintain a positive relationship with your counselor and teachers because you need to be able to access resources when you want to know things to make high school the best time in your life. These people will help to guide you through each class to make sure that your learning style is being used to the maximum ability and that you are receiving the right tools to make you successful.

Not all students learn in the same way. Each person has a more dominant way of learning, which could include visual, auditory, and kinesthetic processes. It is important to know which way you learn best because it will help you to gain more knowledge in the classroom. Do you learn more when you are receiving a lecture from the teacher? Then you would be classified as an auditory learner. If you prefer to learn by reading the text or seeing the assignment via technology or pictures that would classify you as a visual learner. Using your hand to create your learning experience is considered a dominant kinesthetic learner. Often times students use more than one modality to learn, but there is usually a very dominant style that is used more frequently.

When you know what style you learn best you are able to use those methods to understand the lessons. If you have teachers that are not compatible to your learning style there are methods you can use in order to still receive the instruction clearly with great understanding.

One of the best ways to immerse yourself in your education is to attend and encourage your **parent or guardian** to attend ALL Parent/ Guardian events to receive current information regarding high school (Back to School Night, Parent Conferences, Open House, College Night, Testing Informationals, etc.). Parent/guardian nights are designed to keep you informed of the happenings at a school or your own personal progress. This is a time where you can build positive relationships with your teachers and establish a great line of communication with the people that matter the most in your day to day life.

Parent nights are usually scheduled in the evening for the convenience of working families. If this does not fit your families schedule, your parent/guardians should immediately make an appointment at a time that is convenient. Another alternative is to designate a representative who will attend all events if your parent or guardian is not available to meet. This will demonstrate to your teachers that not only are you an advocate for your education, but you have an adult advocate as well.

In secondary education you will need to monitor your progress through report cards throughout the school term. Each high school has a grading policy and procedure that is in alignment with state educational codes. Be sure to know the grading patterns so that you measure the progress through the final reporting period.

Your GPA is based upon a calculated scale on a 4.0 system multiplied by the number of credits you have earned for each class and then divided into the total number of possible credits. This number creates the average that ranks you in comparison to other students in your grade level.

Mentioned earlier in the book is the necessity to maintain a high grade point average (GPA). The minimum GPA of 2.0 is necessary to participate in activities, clubs, and sports teams. However, in order to get accepted in to the college or university of your choice, it is necessary to have a competitive GPA of 3.0 or above.

Colleges across the country may grant you automatic eligibility for entrance when your GPA is a 3.0 or above.

Unsatisfactory "U's" appear on your transcript and are viewed by colleges and universities. CST scores are related to how competitive your school is among other high schools.

Student athletes must abide by the NCAA eligibility rules to qualify for scholarships at participating colleges and universities. In your junior year of high school you must register with the NCAA Clearinghouse at www.ncaaclearinghouse.net.

Division I prospective athletes must complete a total of 16 core-courses, which are closely aligned with the A-G requirements. For Division II the prospective athlete must complete 14 core-courses to become eligible.

The minimum GPA for athletic eligibility is 2.0. However, there is a sliding scale for the SAT or ACT scores based upon the GPA for Division I. The minimum qualifying score for the SAT combined score in math and English only is 820 and for the ACT is a sum of all sections for a minimum total of 68. The writing sections of both tests are not included in the calculation of the score. All scores for the SAT or ACT should be submitted directly to the clearinghouse. The clearinghouse will not accept scores that are posted on the student's transcripts. For more information regarding requirements and eligibility, visit www.ncaa.com and select Prospective Athletes.

What Should Parents/Guardians Know?

To ensure your student is very successful, you must maintain a working relationship with the teachers, counselors, and administration during high school. Students with parents who are involved in their school tend to have fewer behavioral problems and better academic performance, and are more likely to complete secondary school than students whose parents are not involved in their school.[1]

Parents/Guardians have many opportunities to contribute to the student's success during

---

1   Henderson, A.T., and N. Berla. "A New Generation of Evidence: The Family is Critical to Student Achievement." Washington, DC: National Committee for Citizens in Education, 1994.

the entire school year. There are various parent groups on each campus that need governing bodies to make decisions about the school's budget and focus. Additionally, there are Parent Night events at least four times per year. Be proactive and meet with your student's teachers before and after each conferencing period.

Parents/Guardians may visit classrooms for a specified amount of time per class period without communicating with the teacher during instructional time. An appointment with teachers should be made when concerns arise in the classroom. Begin each year with positive intentions in mind.

In the event your child does not follow the steps that have been outlined in the previous chapters of this book and their grades are not passing, there is still hope for earning and graduating with a high school diploma and moving on to college. Remember that the ultimate goal is for your child to succeed. It is possible that the traditional school setting of a comprehensive campus may not be what is best for your child. There are alternative schools like continuation schools and state funded work training programs that are designed to have students complete their basic graduation requirements and to learn a trade. Students who attend alternative schools are still accountable for the state adopted standards, standardized tests, and are still eligible to attend a two year or junior college and transferring to a four year university.

I suggest you examine closely with your child the reasons for not performing to a high level. If it is motivation, then an alternative setting is the best. However, if the student has not grasped the concepts being taught in class it may be necessary to have the student evaluated by a team of professionals at the school to discuss ways to assist the student in the classroom. Some suggestions may be teacher directed or private tutoring, extra-time to complete test or assignments, alternative forms for completing assignments (i.e. video projects and productions versus paper reports), and positive reinforcement in the classroom and at home. In more severe cases, the team may look at providing more formalized assistance with an assessment for special services.

Have an email address available as a contact for teachers and your student's counselor. Keep updated contact information on file at the school to ensure you receive all things via the mail or phone. Ask your child about their work everyday and presume that they had a good day at school. Homework should be given to students in high school totaling two or three hours each day depending on the courses being taken at any one given time. Let the teachers know you are available for your child.

The counselor is also a very important person to have a very good working relationship. The counselor can answer many questions regarding your student's grades, credits, courses, and outside school resources. These are just a few critical things that parents can do to ensure that their student is successful in high school and beyond.

Most schools have a school website that posts up to date information about activities at the school. On some sites teachers are able to post the homework. Be sure to get the website address and visit it frequently to obtain current information.

In the beginning of the year there are various forms that need to be completed. This may happen at registration or the forms may be sent home during the first weeks of school. Be sure to complete each form and return them to the appropriate offices as soon as possible.

Schools receive funding from the federal government for families that meet a certain financial criteria based upon their completed application for free or reducded meal application. This needs to be completed by all parents/guardians and returned to the local district office. Even if you don't qualify it is best to complete this form and return it to the correct offices. You only need one application for multiple school-aged children. When you do qualify for the federal lunch program, your student is eligible for fee waivers for academic tests like the PSAT, SAT and the ACT as well as college application fees. This is a great way to receive all resources for your student.

If you are a parent of a student who has an Individualized Education Plan (IEP) and receives special education services, you must know that many colleges and universities have specialized departments to provide college students with the accommodations outlined in their IEP. Students who are eligible to receive additional time on tests and special directions may also apply for these accommodations when taking the SAT and the ACT for college entrance. Be sure to speak with the counselor or coordinator of special education services about these options for your student if they apply per the IEP.

Another important place for students is the public library. The library is a place where students can find books, magazines, videos, and use the internet for free. When students have reports, projects, or just want to have some free time, the library can be a good place to visit often.

Conclusion

It is with great hope that I covered everything that will allow you to navigate the road to success. I was fortunate to have great people in my life that guided me through each step. I also had the motivation to succeed and utilized the resources I had to graduate from high school, go to the college of my choice, and to ultimately have a career I enjoy.

School can be very fun. With the right attitude and the right choices, there are so many possibilities. Remembering that school is a place to learn you must make an early decision to seek the right information that will benefit you in the future.

I spent four years of working with great high school students who inspired me everyday to do the work I am doing right now. I enjoyed my high school experience so very much that I always wanted to recreate that feeling for my students. As I reflect with my friends from high school, I see that many of our stories are similar. Together we have experienced life with having single parents, divorced parents, violence, two parent households, living with grandparents, living in group homes, yet our stories were profound and have developed some of the greatest people in society.

My Life In 9th Grade

My life as a ninth grade student is very different from life for students now. Ninth grade was junior high school with students in grades 7th – 9th, which is different since schools changed their model to a middle school having students in 6th – 8th grades. When I attended school there were very few schools that had 9th grade students on their campuses. Coincidentally, the high school I attended was one of the pilot schools that had 9th grade students from only one junior high school.

I attended John Burroughs Junior High School of the Los Angeles Unified School District where I was enrolled in the academically challenging courses because I was in the highly gifted magnet. My Algebra and English class counted towards my college entrance requirement. I was a strong student academically because I had mastered using my intelligent mind, but my social activity was very out of whack. I really didn't want to attend the school any longer because I didn't feel like I fit into any crowd though I knew a lot of people. I also was really into liking boys. I wanted to have a boyfriend so badly that my energy was focused on that.

One of the ways that I started to cope with feeling inadequate is I began to ditch classes. A friend and I went to various places in the city instead of remaining at school to attend classes. My reason for ditching is simply I didn't want to be at the school any longer. I didn't feel comfortable with my surroundings because I didn't really like myself. I thought I was too skinny and unattractive, which lowered my self-esteem. I didn't feel good about myself because I hadn't taken much time to get involved in any school activities. During that time the only outside activities that I was involved in was my church choir. Before that I was involved in drill team and a little modeling. I stopped playing the piano and had picked up the talent with "tagging" although the Rapid Transit District, currently known as the Metro, would disagree with my art. Many times I couldn't relate to my mother because she didn't share much of her life with me. What they say is true, "An idol mind is the devil's playing field," and I surely allowed bad types of things to come into my life. I never neglected my studies in school because I had to maintain a façade to my mother that I was doing work in school. I didn't make the connection that some day I would get caught after ditching my sixth period class for nearly a whole semester. My sixth period teacher happened to also be my homeroom teacher. That simple fact should have kept me in class, but it also shows just how determined I was to be away from the place that I didn't enjoy.

I say all of this to help you to understand that had I been involved in more activities I would have enjoyed my experiences in junior high school. My days weren't always bad, but I spent a lot of time focused on the negative aspects even though I was focused enough to maintain my grades making me eligible to participate in culmination. I didn't reach out to anyone about my feelings and how to make my life a better life. I am sure you have friends that are focused on doing negative things. You must be strong for yourself and for them to be a better person and do what you know is right. It will make things better for you and the people around you.

My Life In 10th Grade

"Finally a place that I could call home," is what I felt when I arrived to Washington Preparatory High School in South Los Angeles, CA. I rode the school bus and met a few friends on my bus including a friend from summer school in junior high school. Since I began my high school years in the 10th grade I already had completed courses that counted toward my graduation requirements and college entrance requirements. I had received a "D" on my final spring report card in Algebra due to my truancies, but in summer school I took the class again and received a "B" removing the "D" from my permanent transcript.

I absolutely loved being at The Prep because I had already determined I was ready to get involved into a lot of activities that would help me to enjoy school. My older cousin had recently graduated from the school and had enjoyed her years of attendance. I was determined to take advantage of every opportunity to be the best student including joining the cheerleading squad. One summer I watched the cheerleaders practice at Washington, which motivated me to become a cheerleader too!

The first thing at Washington was getting acquainted with the students in my classes. I was one of the few 10th grade students to have Spanish II because I had taken the first year in junior high school. I really enjoyed Spanish, which motivated me to take three years of the language. I also had a great English teacher who led the academic decathletes to win several awards at Washington and later at Marshall High School.

Our homeroom was the greatest from the very beginning. We were the 10th grade Communication and Arts Magnet students with the last names

A-L. That is where I met and reconnected with my long-time friends. Each one of these ladies reconnected with me through their children when I became an administrator at Westchester High School.

I got acquainted with the administration because our first homeroom teacher Ms. Dickens became the magnet coordinator leaving us to Mrs. Long who has also came back into my life after many years. Our principal, Dr. George McKenna, had a movie about him and the transformation of our school during the early 80's. He and his administrative staff were strong individuals that successfully built a system that fostered the learning of all children. The teachers were dedicated to the well being and uplifting of the students and we truly rose to the occasion of standing for excellence.

I joined a group called the Marthonian, which was the sister club to the Letterman. Both groups provided service to the campus through hosting various events and representing the school for certain activities around campus. The groups were in competition with the Emperors and

Empresses founded by Nita Thomas and the Earls and Earl's Angels. On any given day in October you would see the groups chanting around school competing to see who had the most spirit for their organization. We enjoyed the activities and all participated willingly.

I enjoyed my sophomore year in high school very much. Near the end of the school year cheer try-outs approached. It was my dream to become a cheerleader at Washington Preparatory High School. The students of the school had so much spirit and were so talented that I just had to be apart of this group of ladies.

I first tried out to become a song leader, which was a varsity squad that primarily performed the dance type of routines along with the cheerleaders. This try out was strenuous and usually required more dance abilities than the other squads. After two rounds of cuts I made it to the finals, however, I did not make the squad. That did not deter my ambition because there were cheerleader try-outs the following week. A couple of my friends did make the squad and became great song leaders.

My other friends all tried out for cheer with me. The cheer try outs were a little different because after you made the first cut you were to perform your routine with a select group and the entire school would have an opportunity to vote for you to be on the squad. The first ten selected were varsity and the remaining 8 were junior varsity cheerleaders.

That year the try-outs were very intense. There were more 10th grade students trying out than had before in previous years. If you were going into your senior year you could not be on junior varsity so you were competing for only 10 spots whereas juniors could cheer varsity or junior varsity. There were even three 9th grade students that tried out for cheer this time.

The cheer assembly was held twice to accommodate the total population of the student body. That first assembly was to my detriment when I heard boos from a guy in he audience when my name was called as one of the candidates. My actions that followed were very unpleasant and required me to deal with the consequences.

I was allowed to continue to cheer for the second assembly I am sure to not disrupt the flow of the process, but I had already been disqualified from my participation on the squad. The vote were completed that afternoon and the next few days there was an announcement of the cheerleaders to represent WPHS for the 1988-89 school year. All the names were called and only six junior varsity cheerleaders' names were called when originally it was suppose to be 8. My friend had made the varsity squad along with two other juniors that year. On the junior varsity squad all three ninth grade students' names were called. My name was not call and neither was my other friend's although her performance in my opinion was great.

I was truly heartbroken that I had not made the squad and was very upset when I was later told that I had actually made the squad. Because I made an inappropriate remark during the performance I was disqualified from cheering.

Now you may think that me not being a cheerleader discouraged me from moving on? I was disappointed that my dream was not realized at that point, but I moved forward with my goals of being the most successful student I could be. I joined the Pep squad. The Pep Squad played a very important role filled with lots of Prep Pride.

I also took the PSAT along with other students and friends during my 10th grade year. It was held on a Saturday and you had to pay for your own test. The rooms were filled with students who all decided that this test was important enough for us to take it on a Saturday and we had to pay for it too! Each year we had to take the Write, Sharp and Topics test, which was required to receive your high school diploma and participate in graduation. We just took the test and took it seriously because it was a representation of our character. We really didn't have any clue that it was connected to graduation at that time. At the close of my tenth grade year my GPA was a 3.2 and I was very proud of myself. I loved every aspect of my choice to attend Washington Preparatory High School. There were plenty of parties and fun events throughout the year like

Solid Gold (modeled after the television variety show) and Star Search (a new popular series) that displayed the many talents of our friends.

I attribute my success in the 10th grade to getting involved immediately. Getting involved is the very best thing you can do to ensure that you will have success in high school

My Life In 11th Grade

My eleventh grade year was so amazing. I was on the Pep squad attending all the football games, I was a statistician for the boy's basketball team, and I found more ways to get involved in school.

My friends and I found a nice location on the quad area where we brought a "picnic" blanket to lounge during our break times. We could be seen playing cards (especially UNO) or just enjoying the time together with friends.

My classes were the best with the best teachers. I had pre-calculus, chemistry, history, English, Spanish III, and Speech. These classes were all college preparatory courses that I completed with A's and B's.

I also held a job at McDonald's where I was able to earn extra income to save costs to my family. Working gave me the independence to earn money and be responsible for something other than just going to school. I also started driving in my junior year and inherited my grandfather's work car.

In my junior year I truly challenged myself when I decided to run for Star Search Spokes model competition. There were over 20 candidates competing for two spots in the show. I was selected and another senior. This process included a photo shoot, modeling on stage, and answering a question about social justice and service. That show was so stimulating being that I was a junior competing against a senior. I received numerous applauses and had a marvelous time. Although I didn't win first place, I felt like a winner to even be on stage.

The colleges of my choice were Spellman, NYU, and LMU. I never wanted to attend UCLA or USC because their campuses were too large. My parents were against me going to Spellman because my career goal at the time was to become an attorney. LMU had the best reputation for law. I had visited LMU's campus multiple times and really liked it. Getting to see campus life helped me make my decision.

In my junior year I went to the After Prom. My mother would not allow me to go to the prom because she wanted my first experience to be my own. It was fun to go out with all of my friends and hang out until early in the morning.

Junior year was great, but on to being a Senior.

My Life In 12th Grade

Senior year arrived with lots of fun events. I was a cheerleader, yearbook assistant editor, employed at Mc Donald's, worked the summer at superior court, and taking some rigorous courses to get into college.

My friends and classmates were all working to be their very best in everything. Each day is was common to hear the many college acceptance and financial aid award amounts over the public announcements.

I got my braces off the first day of school, which led to me winning Prettiest Smile in the Senior

Most Competition. I ran for the prom court, but didn't win.

During this time I was very happy with life especially when I was accepted to LMU. I prepared to attend the best school for my career goals. High School was coming to an end, but the memories were long-lasting with lots of fun!

For daily information about how to be a better student visit my blog at http://studentsuccessbybyrd.blogspot.com. If you have any questions that you need answered email me at books@dechelebyrd.com. Enjoy being a great student.

Appendix I
(Getting It Done!)

Get It Done!
9th Grade

To begin your year I suggest you make a list of 4 or more academic goals and 4 or more social goals you plan to achieve during your freshman year in high school. This one process will focus your energy to achieving your goals. Your actions will now become in alignment with creating the outcomes you list on the following pages:

Academic Goals

1. _____

   _____

   _____

   _____

2. _____

   _____

   _____

   _____

3. _____

   _____

   _____

   _____

4. _____

   _____

   _____

   _____

5. _____

   _____

   _____

   _____

Social Goals

1. _____

_____

_____

_____

2. _____

_____

_____

_____

3. _____

_____

_____

_____

4. _____

_____

_____

_____

5. _____

_____

_____

_____

Create a list of the names and email addresses of people who are important in the process of completing your secondary education.

Very Important People (VIPs) around campus:

1. Principal(s), Director(s), Lead Administrator(s): _____

   _____

   _____

   _____

   _____

   _____

   _____

2. Assistant Principal(s), Assistant/Associate Director(s), Co-Administrator(s): _____

   _____

   _____

   _____

   _____

   _____

   _____

3. Dean of Students, Counselor(s), Advisor(s), Other Personnel

: _____

_____

_____

_____

_____

_____

_____

_____

_____

_____

_____

4. Coach(es), Club/Organization Sponsor(s): _____

_____

_____

_____

_____

_____

_____

5. Librarian _____

_____

6. Office Assistant (Attendance or Transcripts): _____

_____

_____

_____

_____

7. Other Campus Personnel _____

_____

_____

_____

_____

_____

_____

_____

_____

_____

_____

Keep your class schedule available to you at all times. Have a copy posted in your locker (if applicable), on your cell phone or PDA, on a bulletin board at home, and most importantly in this guide.

Fall Schedule	Monday	Tuesday	Wednesday	Thursday	Friday
Period 1 Time					
Period 2 Time					
Period 3 Time					
Period 4 Time					
Period 5 Time					
Period 6 Time					
Period 7 Time					
Period 8 Time					

Spring Schedule	Monday	Tuesday	Wednesday	Thursday	Friday
Period 1 Time					
Period 2 Time					
Period 3 Time					
Period 4 Time					
Period 5 Time					
Period 6 Time					
Period 7 Time					
Period 8 Time					

It is always a great idea to follow your daily life with a schedule. This makes your activities deliberate and precise ensuring the most possible success. Below is a sample schedule of a typical teenage student. Create your own and follow it with ever intention.

Sample Tasks	Time
Wake, say morning affirmation, get dressed	6:30 a.m.
Eat a piece of fruit or drink juice	7:00 a.m.
Travel to school	7:10 a.m.
Arrive at school on time	7:50 a.m.
Snack and restroom break	10:00 a.m.
Lunch and restroom break	12:00 p.m.
Travel home	3:00 p.m.
Eat afternoon snack	4:00 p.m.
Begin homework	4:15 p.m.
Chat on the computer with friends	7:00 p.m.
Prepare for the next day	9:30 p.m.
Document accomplishments for the day	9:45 p.m.
Shower and go to bed	10:00 p.m.
Times may vary	

Now create your own schedule being as precise with times as possible.

Tasks	Time

Get It Done!
10th Grade

It is now the 10th grade year and you can reflect on the accomplishment of your goals for the 9th grade. Each year start by making a list of 4 or more academic goals and 4 or more social goals you plan to achieve during your sophomore year in high school. This one process will focus your energy to achieving your goals. Your actions will now become in alignment with creating the outcomes you list on the following pages:

Academic Goals

1. _____

   _____

   _____

   _____

2. _____

   _____

   _____

   _____

3. _____

   _____

   _____

   _____

4. _____

   _____

   _____

   _____

5. _____

   _____

   _____

   _____

Social Goals

1. _____

_____

_____

_____

2. _____

_____

_____

_____

3. _____

_____

_____

_____

4. _____

_____

_____

_____

5. _____

_____

_____

_____

Fall Schedule	Monday	Tuesday	Wednesday	Thursday	Friday
Period 1 Time					
Period 2 Time					
Period 3 Time					
Period 4 Time					
Period 5 Time					
Period 6 Time					
Period 7 Time					
Period 8 Time					

Spring Schedule	Monday	Tuesday	Wednesday	Thursday	Friday
Period 1 Time					
Period 2 Time					
Period 3 Time					
Period 4 Time					
Period 5 Time					
Period 6 Time					
Period 7 Time					
Period 8 Time					

In the 10th grade you must know about your progress. Answer the following questions and review them on a regular basis to be very happy about your accomplishments:

1. What is your overall Grade Point Average? _____

    _____

2. What is your favorite subject? _____

    _____

3. Who do you hang out with the most and why? _____

    _____

    _____

    _____

    _____

    _____

    _____

    _____

4. What is your score on the PSAT, Explore, or other preparation test? _____

    _____

----

5.   What areas do you want to improve for this year? _____

----

6.   What activities did you participate in that you enjoyed? _

----

7. What is the best thing about being in high school? Why? _

Get It Done!
11th Grade

Two years have gone by with great success on your behalf. As we continue to build your greatness challenge yourself this year to doing bigger and better goals by making a list of 4 or more academic goals and 4 or more social goals you plan to achieve during your junior year in high school.

Academic Goals

1. _____

   _____

   _____

   _____

2. _____

   _____

   _____

   _____

3. _____

   _____

   _____

   _____

4. _____

   _____

   _____

   _____

5. _____

   _____

   _____

   _____

Social Goals

1. _____

_____

_____

_____

2. _____

_____

_____

_____

3. _____

_____

_____

_____

4. _____

_____

_____

_____

5. _____

_____

_____

_____

Keep a record of your class schedule and the times that each class meets. Your schedule is an important way to keep the pace on being successful. Remember to keep it posted in the places that you use the most like your notebook, locker (if applicable) and your mirror at home.

Fall Schedule	Monday	Tuesday	Wednesday	Thursday	Friday
Period 1 Time					
Period 2 Time					
Period 3 Time					
Period 4 Time					
Period 5 Time					
Period 6 Time					
Period 7 Time					
Period 8 Time					

Spring Schedule	Monday	Tuesday	Wednesday	Thursday	Friday
Period 1 Time					
Period 2 Time					
Period 3 Time					
Period 4 Time					
Period 5 Time					
Period 6 Time					
Period 7 Time					
Period 8 Time					

Changes may have taken place in your life because you have a job or have practice for a sport or activity that requires more time for you to plan your schedule. Below update your schedule to ensure that you have time to complete all the important things in your life.

Tasks	Time

In the eleventh grade you will begin to narrow your choices for college options or career programs. Describe your post-secondary options for when you graduate from high school.

_____

_____

_____

_____

_____

_____

_____

_____

_____

_____

_____

_____

_____

_____

_____

_____

_____

_____

_____

_____

_____

_____

_____

_____

_____

_____

List the colleges or universities you are interested in attending:

1. _____

_____

_____

_____

_____

2. _____

_____

_____

_____

----

3. --

----

4. --

----

5. --

Use the calendar below to schedule campus visits. Plan your dates so that students are in session at the colleges you wish to see.

Sun	Mon	Tue	Wed	Thu	Fri	Sat

Get It Done!
12th Grade

It is senior year and there is so much to organize. Take time to complete this list to stay focused on having a very smooth year.

1. How many credits to you have now? _____

   _____

2. What courses do you need to take to complete your

   senior year? _____

   _____

   _____

   _____

_____

_____

_____

_____

_____

3. What is your Grade Point Average (GPA)? _____

_____

_____

4. Which colleges or universities do you plan to apply for

    admissions?   _____

_____

_____

_____

_____

_____

_____

_____

_____

5. Have you taken the SAT or the ACT exams? If so, what

is your score? _____

_____

_____

_____

_____

_____

6. If you have not taken the SAT or the ACT, have you
   registered for the test in October? _____

   _____

7. List the names of four adults to write letters of
   recommendations for your college applications. _____

   _____

   _____

   _____

   _____

   _____

   _____

   _____

   _____

_____

_____

_____

8. Help your parents/guardians get their financial information available for the March 2nd due date for filing your Federal Application For Student Aid (FAFSA).

9. When is your senior portrait appointment? _____

_____

_____

10. What are your payment dates for you senior package?

_____

_____

_____

_____

_____

11. Describe your ideal prom scenario. Be sure to use specific details including the color of your dress and who your date will be. _____

_____

----

12. Create a list of people to send announcements of your graduation at least four weeks in advanced.

13. What college(s) or universities did you get accepted into?

_____

_____

_____

_____

_____

_____

_____

_____

_____

_____

_____

_____

_____

_____

14. How many scholarships were you awarded? _____

_____

_____

_____

_____

_____

_____

_____

_____

_____

15. What career are you interested in having you're your life?

_____

_____

_____

_____

_____

_____

_____

_____

_____

16. What preparation besides college is necessary to have

this career? _____

_____

_____

_____

_____

_____

_____

_____

_____

17. Tell about the accomplishments you made during your

high school years. _____

_____

_____

_____

_____

_____

_____

_____

_____

_____

_____

_____

_____

_____

_____

_____

_____

_____

_____

_____

_____

_____

_____

_____

_____

_____

_____

Now it is time to create more lasting memories.
Congratulations!